AF353000

Colección: Libros de inglés para Infantil y Primaria

CUENTOS Y POESÍAS EN INGLÉS
PARA INFANTIL 3 AÑOS

I CAN SLEEP ALONE! I'M GROWING! (FAMILY)

"YES, I DO." (SCHOOL)

GOOD BEHAVIOR IN THE LIVING ROOM (TOYS)

LET'S GO TO THE PARK (CLOTHES)

EAT FRUIT AND VEGETABLES EVERY DAY (FOOD)

I AM NOT AFRAID OF SWIMMING POOLS (SUMMER)

MY FIRST BIRTHDAY PARTY WITH MY FRIENDS
(BIRTHDAY)

LET'S COUNT THE STARS (CHRISTMAS AND THE
THREE WISE MEN)

TICKLING SENSATION AND ROLLING EGGS (EASTER)

THE DINOSAUR ISLAND (ANIMALS)

EAT EVERYTHING! (FOOD)

'CAN I HELP YOU?' (ATTITUDE)

Copyright © Pilar Bellés Pitarch, 2014
1ª edición: agosto 2014
ISBN: 978-84-617-1331-8
Depósito Legal: CS-267-2014

Pilar Bellés Pitarch (1964). Es licenciada en Filología Inglesa y profesora de inglés. Hace años que se dedica a investigar sobre las posibilidades del cuento para desarrollar la creatividad y trabajar valores. También cuenta con investigaciones sobre métodos para aprender inglés.

Estos son los cuentos y poesías que usa en sus clases de inglés. Cada cuento tiene sus imágenes en color y su poema. A los niños de esta edad les gusta recitar poemas en lengua extranjera y así, mientras escuchan el cuento en inglés interactúan y usan la lengua.

Son de gran utilidad tanto para los profesores o profesoras de inglés como para los padres y madres que quieran mejorar el nivel de inglés de sus hijos o hijas.

Pilar Bellés cuenta además con numerosas publicaciones en cuento, novela y poesía.

Publicaciones sobre cuentos plurilingües y valores en el campo de la enseñanza:

•"Telling a tale / Contemos un cuento / Contem un conte" (adaptados a los centros de interés de educación infantil).

• "Cuentos plurilingües para trabajar valores y para días especiales" (día del árbol, día de la paz, Halloween…)

•"¿Cómo hacer alumnos creativos?" (cuentos plurilingües para desarrollar la creatividad y, a la vez, trabajar valores para todas las edades).

• "No dejes que crezca sin la magia de los cuentos… según lo que quieras transmitir, elige un cuento y… cuéntaselo" (alternativa a los cuentos tradicionales).

Métodos para aprender inglés a través de la literatura:

•"Els iaios, la natura i l'amor / Los abuelos, la naturaleza y el amor / Grandparents, Love and Nature" (método de las historias plurilingües).

•"Federico y su duende / Frederick and his Goblin" (método de las historias bilingües).

Novela:

•"El diario mágico" (contra la violencia de género). Ediciones Carena.

•"Somos víctimas de una sociedad machista y cruel" (contra el machismo y la desigualdad). Ediciones Grup Lobher.

•"El mensaje" (contra el acoso y la manipulación). Ediciones Carena.

•"La rosa deshojada" (contra la violencia de género) de Pilar Bellés y Maribel Rueda. JNQ Ediciones.

•"Triunfar en tiempos difíciles" con el método de los relatos interrelacionados. JNQ Ediciones.

."Reunión de colegas" (se nos manipula sin que nos demos cuenta…). Editorial Lulu.

Biografía:
. "Toda una vida: memorias y anécdotas de Mel y Xispa". De Manuel Falcó García (Xispa) y Pilar Bellés Pitarch. Editorial viveLibro.

. Teatro: "Engaño perfecto". Editorial Lulu.

. Poesía: "Curvas en el camino". Ediciones Carena.

. Ensayo: "Educar en valores actuales a través de la literatura y otros ensayos". Editorial Lulu.

I CAN SLEEP ALONE! I'M GROWING!
(FAMILY)

WHEN HE WAS A BABY, HE LIKED SLEEPING IN MUM'S
ARMS. HE FELL ASLEEP AND MUM PUT HIM IN HIS COT.
IF HER BABY WAS NERVOUS, MUM TOUCHED HIS
HAND TO CALM HIM.
THE PROBLEM BEGAN WHEN THE COT IS TOO SMALL
FOR HIM AND THE CHILD MUST GO TO HIS BED.
MUM TELLS HIM A TALE.
'DON'T GO!' SAYS THE CHILD. 'I NEED YOUR HAND TO
SLEEP.'
'OK, BUT THEN YOU MUST SLEEP THE WHOLE NIGHT.'

BABY, BABY, BABY

COT, COT, COT

SLEEP WITH MUM

YES, YES, YES.

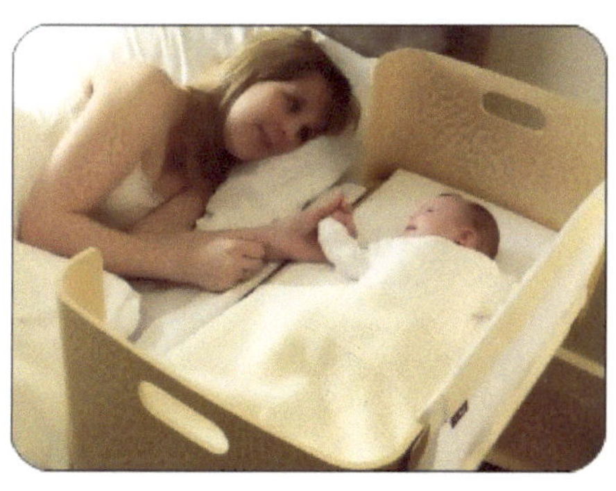

THE CHILD SLEEPS BUT, WHEN MUM AND DAD GO TO BED AND FALL ASLEEP, HE GOES TO THEIR BED AND HE LIES DOWN BETWEEN THEM.
'OH NO! WHAT ARE YOU DOING?' ASKS DAD.
'I'M SCARED. ONLY THIS NIGHT, PLEASE…'
THAT HAPPENS EVERY NIGHT. MUM AND DAD ARE SAD.

SLEEP ALONE
OH, OH!
GO TO MUM'S BED
YES, YES, YES.

SUMMER ARRIVES. IT IS VERY HOT AT NIGHT. WHEN MUM AND DAD FALL ASLEEP THE CHILD WALKS TO THEIR BED AND HE LIES DOWN BETWEEN THEM.
THE BED IS VERY HOT AND WET. HE IS TERRIBLY HOT. HE GOES TO HIS BED. IT IS WARM. HE SLEEPS FINE IN HIS OWN BED WHERE HE IS NOT HOT. IT IS THE BEST NIGHT OF HIS LIFE.
THE NEXT DAY:
'MUM, I SLEPT VERY WELL AND COMFORTABLE.

MUM'S BED
HOT, HOT, HOT,
MY BEDROOM
OK, OK, OK.

9

THE BOY HAS SOMETHING TO SAY:
'I WANT TO SLEEP IN MY OWN BED… IT'S THE MOST COMFORTABLE PLACE IN THE WORLD.'
'ARE YOU AFRAID OF THE DARK?'
'NO, IT IS NONSENSE…' SAYS THE CHILD.
'OUR CHILD IS GROWING!' SAYS MUM.
'YES, I THINK SO.'
THE CHILD IS VERY HAPPY:
'I'M GROWING! HURRAY!'
THE CHILD SLEEPS ALONE. ACCORDING TO HIS EXPERIENCE, IT IS THE BEST OPTION. BUT ONCE A WEEK, ON SATURDAYS OR ON SUNDAYS HE GOES TO HIS PARENT'S BED AND HE PLAYS WITH THEM.

I LIKE MY BEDROOM
HAPPY, HAPPY, HAPPY,
I CAN SLEEP ALONE
ONE, TWO, THREE.

I CAN SLEEP ALONE!

BABY, BABY, BABY
COT, COT, COT
SLEEP WITH MUM
YES, YES, YES.

SLEEP ALONE
OH, OH!
GO TO MUM'S BED
YES, YES, YES.

MUM'S BED
HOT, HOT, HOT,
MY BEDROOM
OK, OK, OK.

I LIKE MY BEDROOM
HAPPY, HAPPY, HAPPY,
I CAN SLEEP ALONE
ONE, TWO, THREE.

"YES, I DO."
(SCHOOL)

THERE WAS A SMALL LION. HE HAS GOT A PROBLEM: WHEN MUM AND DAD ASK HIM TO DO SOMETHING, HE ALWAYS ANSWERS THE SAME:
'NO, I DON'T.'
THEY REPRIMAND HIM, THEY PUNISH HIM. BUT HIS BEHAVIOUR DOESN'T CHANGE.
HE GOES TO SCHOOL. THE TEACHER SAYS:
'SIT DOWN AND TAKE THE PENCIL'
'NO, I DON'T,' SAYS HE.
 SHE REPRIMANDS HIM.
'OK, YES, I DO.'
THE SAME HAPPENS WITH THE RUBBER, PAPERS, GLUE AND SCISSORS.

SIT DOWN,
NO, I DON'T.
PUNISHMENT!
YES, I DO.
TAKE THE PENCIL…

BEFORE GOING TO BED HE MUST GO TO THE TOILET.
'GO TO THE TOILET, SWEET, PLEASE,' SAYS MUM.
'NO, I DON'T,' SAYS HE.
'PUNISHMENT!'
'OK, OK. YES, I DO.'
THE SAME HAPPENS WITH GOING TO BED.

GO TO THE TOILET
NO, I DON'T
PUNISHMENT!
YES, I DO.

GO TO BED
NO, I DON'T
PUNISHMENT!
YES, I DO.

IT IS LUNCHTIME.
'SIT DOWN AND HAVE LUNCH' SAYS DAD.
'NO, I DON'T,' SAYS THE SMALL LION.
'PUNISHMENT!'
'OK, OK. YES, I DO.'
THE SAME STORY IS REPEATED FOR THE NAP TIME.
HE DOESN'T OBEY THE FIRST TIME.

HAVE LUNCH
NO, I DON'T
PUNISHMENT!
YES, I DO.

TAKE A NAP
NO, I DON'T
PUNISHMENT!
YES, I DO.

ONCE THERE IS A BIRTHDAY. THERE'S A BIG CAKE. THE SMALL LION LIKES PARTIES AND CAKES.

'GO TO THE TABLE AND HAVE A PIECE OF CAKE,' SAYS THE TEACHER.

'NO, I DON'T,' SAYS HE.

'OK.'

THE TEACHER DOESN'T REPEAT THE ORDER. HE GOES ON PLAYING. MEANWHILE THE REST OF STUDENTS EAT ALL THE CAKE.

THE SMALL LION IS WAITING… BUT, WHAT IS HAPPENING? WHAT A SURPRISE! THERE IS NO CAKE.

THE SMALL LION LEARNS THE LESSON. SINCE THEN HE OBEYS THE FIRST TIME.

HE BECAME A WELL-MANNERED LION AND THEY LIVED HAPPILY ALL THEIR LIVES.

OBEY, OBEY
THE FIRST TIME
ALWAYS SAY
YES, I DO.

YES, I DO

SIT DOWN,
NO, I DON'T.
PUNISHMENT!
OK. YES, I DO.

TAKE YOUR PENCIL
NO, I DON'T.
PUNISHMENT!
OK. YES, I DO.

GO TO THE TOILET
NO, I DON'T
PUNISHMENT!
OK. YES, I DO.

GO TO BED
NO, I DON'T
PUNISHMENT!
OK. YES, I DO.

OBEY, OBEY
THE FIRST TIME
ALWAYS SAY
YES, I DO.

GOOD BEHAVIOR IN THE LIVING ROOM
(TOYS)

IT WAS THE SUMMER HOLIDAYS. THE SMALL BOY IS AT HOME WITH MUM AND DAD. HE IS PLAYING IN THE LIVING ROOM.   HE HAS GOT A LOT OF TOYS.

I PLAY WITH MY TOYS
A CAR, A BALL, A DRUM.
A KITE, A BALLOON, A TRAIN,
A BOAT AND A TEDDY BEAR.

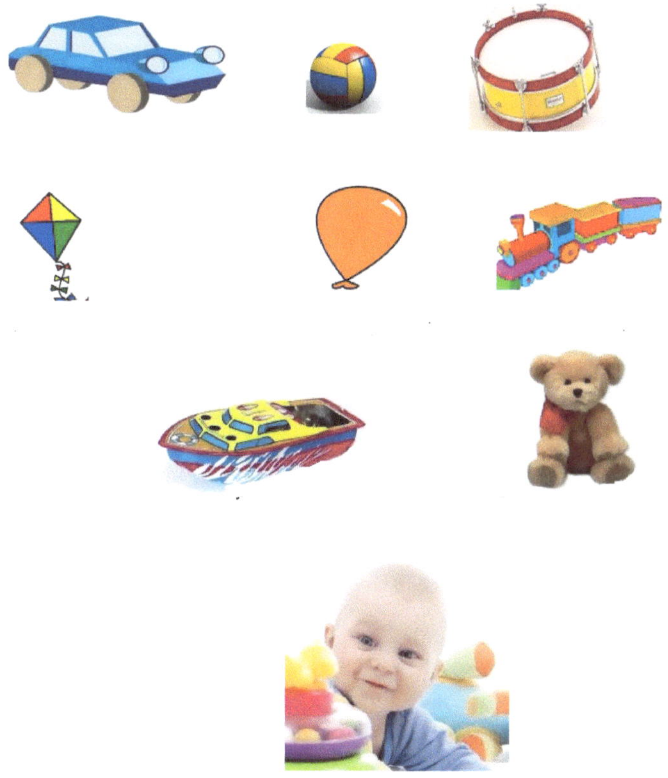

HE USUALLY PLAYS QUIETLY, BUT TODAY HE IS NAUGHTY. HE IS BEHAVING BADLY IN THE LIVING ROOM.
FIRST HE THROWS AWAY ALL THE CUSHIONS AND THEN HE PLAYS FOOTBALL WITH THEM. THEN HE GETS OUT ALL THE TOYS FROM THEIR BOXES. IT IS A MESS.
MUM REPRIMANDS HIM FOR IT. THEN HE PUTS THE TOYS INTO THEIR BOXES.

BAD BEHAVIOUR,
OH NO! OH NO!
PICK UP YOUR TOYS,
YES, YES, YES.

WHEN MUM GOES OUT OF THE LIVING ROOM HE DROPS THE BALLS ON THE FLOOR, IN THE SOFA, UNDER THE TABLE… EVERYWHERE.
WHEN MUM FINISHES THE HOUSEWORK SHE IS VERY TIRED. SHE SITS ON THE SOFA, BUT UNFORTUNATELY SHE SLIPS ON A SMALL BALL AND SHE FALLS ON THE FLOOR. SHE IS SLEEPING FOR A WHILE…
THE SMALL BOY COVERS HER WITH A BLANKET AND HE PUTS A CUSHION UNDER HER HEAD TO REST ON.
WHEN MUM WAKES UP SHE SEES ALL THE TOYS IN THEIR BOXES AND ALL THE BALLS IN THEIR BAG.
'SORRY, MUM,' SAYS THE SMALL BOY WHEN SHE OPENS HER EYES. 'ARE YOU TIRED?'
SHE TAKES HIM IN HER ARMS. HE CHANGED HIS BEHAVIOUR AND HE TIDIED UP HIS TOYS. THEY LIVED HAPPILY EVER AFTER.

MUM IS SLEEPING
OH NO! OH NO!
GOOD BEHAVIOUR
ONE, TWO, TREE.

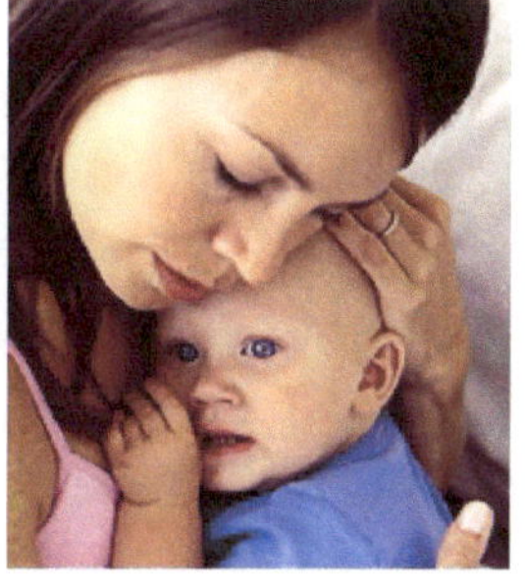

GOOD BEHAVIOUR

I PLAY WITH MY TOYS
A CAR, A BALL, A DRUM.
A KITE, A BALLOON, A TRAIN,
A BOAT AND A TEDDY BEAR.

BAD BEHAVIOUR,
OH NO! OH NO!
PICK UP YOUR TOYS,
YES, YES, YES.

MUM IS SLEEPING
OH NO! OH NO!
GOOD BEHAVIOUR
YES, YES, YES,
YOU ARE HAPPY
ONE, TWO, TREE.

LET'S GO TO THE PARK
(CLOTHES)

THE SMALL BOY LIKES GOING TO THE PARK WITH GRANNY, GRANDAD, MUM AND DAD.   HE LIKES SWINGS BUT SOME-TIMES HE GOES TO THE SLIDE, THE CASTLE OR THE SEESAWING, UP AND DOWN. HE PREFERS THE SWINGS.
IN SUMMER AND AUTUMN HE WEARS A T-SHIRT, TROUSERS AND SHOES AND HE GOES TO THE PARK EVERY DAY.

GOING TO THE PARK
YES, YES, YES
IN SUMMER AND AUTUMN
T-SHIRT, TROUSERS AND SHOES.

T-SHIRT   TROUSERS   SHOES

ONE WINTER DAY, HE IS WEARING A HAT, GLOVES, SCARF, JACKET AND SWEATER. IT IS RAINING CONTINUOUSLY AND THEY CAN'T GO TO THE PARK. THEY MUST STAY AT HOME. HE IS PLAYING WITH THE SAME TOYS ALL DAY. HE DOESN'T WANT TO SHARE HIS TOYS, BUT HE IS BORED, TERRIBLY BORED.
HIS NEIGHBOUR'S SMALL CHILD HAS GOT THE SAME PROBLEM.
'CAN WE PLAY TOGETHER AND SHARE OUR TOYS?, DAD.'
'YES, YOU CAN,' SAYS DAD.
IN THIS WAY THEY PLAY TOGETHER AND THEY HAVE A NICE TIME.

WINTER, WINTER,
HAT, GLOVES, SCARF,
JACKET AND SWEATER
SHARE YOUR TOYS
YES, YES, YES

HAT GLOBES SCARF   JACKET   SWEATER

AFTER THAT THEY PLAY TOGETHER AT HOME OR THEY GO TO THE PARK ONCE OR TWICE A WEEK. THEY GO ON THE SWINGS OR THEY PLAY OTHER GAMES. HE LIKES PLAYING WITH MUM AND DAD TOO. PLAYING TOGETHER IS A NICE EXPERIENCE.

PLAY TOGETHER
YES, YES, YES
PLAY WITH MUM AND DAD
YOU ARE HAPPY
ONE, TWO, THREE.

LET'S GO TO THE PARK

GOING TO THE PARK
YES, YES, YES
IN SUMMER AND AUTUMN
T-SHIRT, TROUSERS AND SHOES.

WINTER, WINTER,
HAT, GLOVES, SCARF,
JACKET AND SWEATER
SHARE YOUR TOYS
YES, YES, YES

PLAY TOGETHER
YES, YES, YES
PLAY WITH MUM AND DAD
YOU ARE HAPPY
ONE, TWO, THREE.

ONE DOG, TWO DUCKS, THREE CATS.
(BODY AND ANIMALS)

IT IS TIME FOR THE AFTERNOON SANDWICH. CHILDREN GO TO THE PARK WITH THEIR PETS. PETER HAS GOT A PUPPY.
THE PUPPY HAS GOT ONE HEAD, ONE BODY, FOUR LEGS AND ONE TAIL. HE CAN STAND UP, SIT DOWN, RUN AND TURN AROUND.

PETER'S GOT ONE DOG,
ONE BODY, ONE HEAD,
A TAIL, FOUR LEGS.
STAND UP, SIT DOWN
RUN AND TURN AROUND.

STAND UP

SIT DOWN

RUN AND TURN AROUND

JOHN HAS GOT TWO DUCKLINGS. THEY ARE YELLOW. THEY HAVE GOT ONE HEAD, ONE BODY AND TWO LEGS. THEY'VE GOT BEAK AND FEATHERS. THEY ARE THE CAT FRIENDS.

JOHN HAS GOT
TWO YELLOW DUCKINGS
ONE, TWO
HEAD, BODY AND LEGS
BEAK AND FEATHERS TOO.
WHAT CAN THEY DO?

DUCKINGS

BEAK

FEATHERS

MARY HAS GOT THREE CATS; ONE BIG CAT AND TWO SMALL ONES. MUM IS BIG. SHE HAS GOT A BIG HEAD, A BIG BODY AND FOUR BIG LEGS. HER KITTENS ARE SMALL. ONE KITTEN IS BROWN AND THE OTHER KITTEN IS BLACK. THEY HAVE GOT SMALL HEADS, SMALL BODIES AND SMALL LEGS.

MARY'S GOT THREE CATS,
ONE, TWO, THREE
MUM IS BIG
SHE'S GOT BIG HEAD,
BIG BODY AND BIG LEGS.
THE KITTENS ARE SMALL
THEY'VE GOT SMALL HEAD.
SMALL BODY AND SMALL LEGS.

PUPPY

KITTEN

DUCKING

HAMSTER

RABBIT

CHICK

HEN

PIGLET

LAMB

ONE DOG, TWO DUCKS, THREE CATS

PETER'S GOT ONE DOG,
ONE BODY, ONE HEAD,
A TAIL, FOUR LEGS.
STAND UP, SIT DOWN
RUN AND TURN AROUND.

JOHN HAS GOT
TWO YELLOW DUCKS
ONE, TWO
HEAD, BODY AND LEGS
BEAK AND FEATHERS TOO.
WHAT CAN THEY DO?

MARY'S GOT THREE CATS,
ONE, TWO, THREE
MUM IS BIG
SHE'S GOT BIG HEAD,
BIG BODY AND BIG LEGS.
THE KITTENS ARE SMALL
THEY'VE GOT SMALL HEAD.
SMALL BODY AND SMALL LEGS.

HAVE YOU GOT A PET?
YES, YES, YES
YOU ARE HAPPY
ONE, TWO, THREE.

EAT FRUIT AND VEGETABLES EVERY DAY
(FOOD)

THERE IS A VEGETARIAN FISH. HE LIKES VEGETABLES BUT HE CAN'T GET THEM. IT IS DIFFICULT FOR HIM. HE IS IN THE WATER AND VEGETABLES ARE OUT OF THE WATER. HE SEES A RABBIT EATING FRUIT AND VEGETABLES. HE LOOKS AT THE RABBIT.
THE RABBIT SEES HIM.
'CAN I HELP YOU? WHAT ARE YOU LOOKING FOR?' ASKS THE RABBIT.
'I WOULD LIKE TO HAVE SOME VEGETABLES…'
'HERE YOU ARE.'
'DELICIOUS!'

RABBIT, RABBIT
HAPPY, HAPPY,
FRUIT AND VEGETABLES EVERY DAY
DELICIOUS!
FISH, FISH, FISH
SAD, SAD, SAD
NO FRUIT AND VEGETABLES
NO, NO, NO.

'WHAT DO YOU WANT?' SAYS THE RABBIT.
'I WANT SOME PARSLEY, PLEASE,' SAYS THE FISH.
THE RABBIT GIVES HIM PURSLEY LEAVE.
'THANK YOU,' SAYS THE FISH AND HE EATS IT.
THE NEXT DAY:
'I WANT SOME LETTUCE, ' SAYS THE FISH.
THE RABBIT GIVES HIM SOME LETTUCE.
'THANK YOU,'
IN THIS WAY THE FISH EATS VEGETABLES EVERY DAY.

PARSLEY, PARSLEY
DELICIOUS!
LETTUCE, LETTUCE
DELICIOUS!

THE NEXT DAY:
ANYTHING ELSE?' ASKS RABBIT.
'BANANA, PLEASE,' PLEASE.
THE RABBIT GIVES HIM A BANANA.
THE NEXT DAY:
'CAN I HAVE SOME ORANGE, PLEASE?'
HERE YOU ARE.

I LIKE BANANA
DELICIOUS!
I LIKE ORANGE
DELICIOUS!

CAN I HAVE VEGETABLES AND FRUIT EVERYDAY?'
ASKS THE FISH.
'YES, OF COURSE,' SAYS THE RABBIT.
'EVERY DAY I'LL GIVE YOU SOME LEAVES OF
DIFFERENT VEGETABLES AND SOME FRUIT. MUM
SAYS THAT FOOD MUST BE VARIED…'
THE FISH AND THE RABBIT ARE FRIENDS. THEY EAT
VEGETABLES AND FRUIT EVERY DAY. HE IS HEALTHY
AND STRONG. THEY ARE VERY HAPPY.

FRUIT AND VEGETABLES
HEALTHY AND STRONG
WE ARE HAPPY
ONE, TWO, THREE.

DO YOU LIKE FRUIT AND VEGETABLES?

EAT FRUIT AND VEGETABLES EVERY DAY

RABBIT, RABBIT
HAPPY, HAPPY,
FRUIT AND VEGETABLES EVERY DAY
DELICIOUS!

FISH, FISH, FISH
SAD, SAD, SAD
NO FRUIT AND VEGETABLES
NO, NO, NO

PARSLEY, PARSLEY
DELICIOUS!
LETTUCE, LETTUCE
DELICIOUS!

I LIKE BANANA
DELICIOUS!
I LIKE ORANGE
DELICIOUS!

FRUIT AND VEGETABLES
HEALTHY AND STRONG
WE ARE HAPPY
ONE, TWO, THREE.

I AM NOT AFRAID OF SWIMMING POOLS
(SUMMER)

'LET'S GO TO THE SWIMMING POOL,' SAYS MUM.
'NO, I DON'T,' SAYS THE SMALL GIRL 'I'M AFRAID.'
'LET'S GO ON A SHIP,' SAYS MUM.
'OK,' SAYS THE SMALL GIRL

SWIMMING POOL
NO, NO, NO
GO ON A SHIP
YES, YES, YES

SHE PLAYS WITH OTHER BOYS AND GIRLS. THEN,
THEY GO INTO THE POOL BUT SHE DOESN'T.
"WHAT CAN WE DO?"
MUM WAITS…
A TIME LATER, THE SMALL GIRL DECIDES TO GO INTO
THE POOL MUM GOES INTO THE POOL WITH HER.
'WATER IS HOT. I LIKE IT,' SAYS THE GIRL.
'YES, I THINK SO,' SAYS MUM.
SHE LIKES THE SENSATION OF WATER ON HER LEGS.
WATER IS CLEAR AND SOFT.

PLAY, PLAY, PLAY
YES, YES, YES
GO INTO THE POOL
YES, YES, YES

 HIS FRIENDS ARRIVE AND THEY GO INTO THE SWIMMING POOL TOO. THEY PLAY FOR A LONG TIME.
IT'S TIME FOR THE AFTERNOON BREAK.
'SWEET, THE SANDWICH!,' SAY MUMS.
THEY GOT OUT, THEY EAT THE AFTERNOON SANDWICH AND THEY PLAY.
'I AM NOT AFRAID OF SWIMIMINGPOOLS, MUM,' SAYS THE SMALL GIRL.
'I'M PROUD OF YOU,' SAYS MUM.
THE SMALL GIRL IS VERY HAPPY PLAYING WITH HER FRIENDS AT THE SWIMMING POOL.

PLAY IN THE POOL
YES, YES, YES
HAPPY, HAPPY
ONE, TWO, THREE.

I'M NOT AFRAID OF SWIMMING POOLS

SWIMMING POOL
NO, NO, NO
GO ON A SHIP
YES, YES, YES

PLAY, PLAY, PLAY
YES, YES, YES
GO INTO THE POOL
YES, YES, YES

PLAY IN THE POOL
YES, YES, YES
YOU ARE HAPPY
ONE, TWO, THREE.

MY FIRST BIRTHDAY PARTY WITH MY FRIENDS
(BIRTHDAY)

JOHN IS THREE TODAY. IT IS HIS FIRST BIRTHDAY PARTY AT HOME WITH HIS SCHOOL FRIENDS. EVERY FRIEND COMES WITH A BIG PRESENT.
'HAPPY BIRTHDAY! HERE YOU ARE!'
'THANK YOU!' HE SAYS.
HE OPENS MORE AND MORE PRESENTS AND PUTS HIS NEW TOYS IN A SHELF: A CAR, A TRAIN, A PLAIN, A ROBOT, A KITE, A BIG BALLOON, A BALL… (STUDENTS REVIEW TOYS).

JOHN IS THREE TODAY
A BIRTHDAY CAKE
BIG, BIG, BIG
A BIRTHDAY PARTY
JOHN IS HAPPY

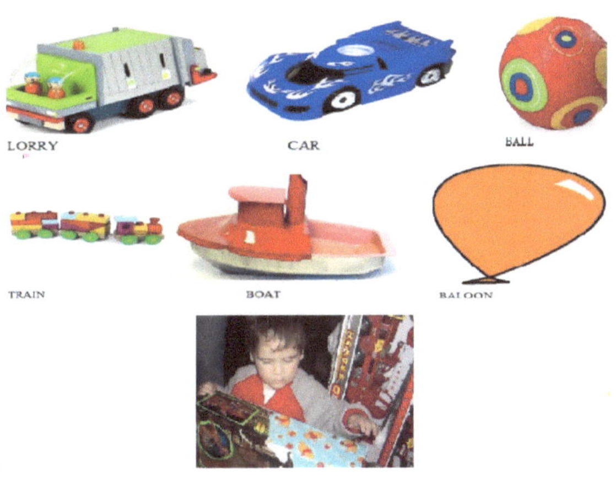

THERE IS A BIG TABLE WITH ALL KIND OF FOOD: SANDWICHES, LEMONADE, JUICE, BISCUITS, CHIPS, FRUIT…
THERE IS NICE MUSIC. THERE ARE STREAMERS AND BALLOONS EVERYWHERE.
THERE ARE CLOWNS AND GAMES FOR CHILDREN. THEY ARE GREAT! THERE ARE BAGS WITH SWEETS FOR EVERYBODY.

A BIG TABLE
WITH SANDWICHES
AND LEMONADE,
BAGS OF SWEETS
AND CLOWNS WITH GAMES.

THEN, THE BIRTHDAY CAKE. EVERYBODY SINGS "HAPPY BIRTHDAY TO YOU". HE BLOWS OUT THE CANDLES AND HE MAKES A WISH.
WHAT A NICE CAKE! TWO HOURS TO REMEMBER FOR ALL HIS LIFE. WHAT A NICE PARTY!
'IT'S THE BEST PARTY IN THE WORLD, MUM AND DAD,' SAYS HE. 'MUM, DAD…I LOVE YOU.'
HE WILL HAVE LOTS OF PARTIES TO HAVE FUN WITH HIS FRIENDS, BUT THE FIRST BIRTHDAY PARTY IS THE BEST!

MY FIRST BIRTHDAY PARTY
HAPPY, HAPPY, HAPPY,
THANK YOU MUM AND DAD
ONE, TWO, THREE.

Y FIRST BIRTHDAY PARTY WITH FRIENDS

JOHN IS THREE TODAY
A BIRTHDAY CAKE
BIG, BIG, BIG
A BIRTHDAY PARTY
JOHN IS HAPPY

A BIG TABLE
WITH SANDWICHES
AND LEMONADE,
BAGS OF SWEETS
AND CLOWNS WITH GAMES.

MY FIRST BIRTHDAY PARTY
HAPPY, HAPPY, HAPPY,
THANK YOU MUM AND DAD
ONE, TWO, THREE.

LET'S COUNT THE STARS
(CHRISTMAS AND THE THREE WISE MEN)

ONCE UPON A TIME THERE WAS A CHILD THAT COULDN'T SLEEP. IT WAS CHRISTMAS HOLIDAY AND HE WAITED FOR *THE THREE WISE MEN*'S ARRIVAL.
HE CLOSES HIS EYES AND HE IMAGINES A GREEN LIGHT DIVIDED INTO FIVE SMALL LIGHTS.
'IS THE GREEN LIGHT THE STAR OF BETHLEHEM?' ASKS THE SMALL BOY.
'THE STAR OF BETHLEHEM HAS GOT A TAIL…,' SAYS MUM.
'OK. I'LL TRY AGAIN…'

THE THREE WISE MEN
EMOTION, EMOTION
I CAN SLEEP
LET'S COUNT THE STARS.

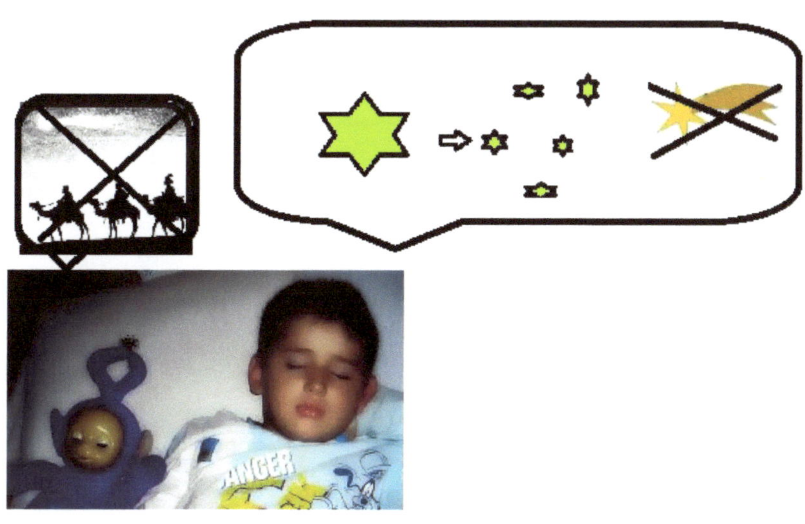

HE IS RIDING A WHITE HORSE THAT JUMPS AND JUMPS: "ONE, TWO, THREE…"
HE SEES A BLUE LIGHT AND A RED ONE. BOTH OF THEM DIVIDE INTO NEW STARS.
'ARE THESE THE STARS OF BETHLEHEM?'
'NO, THEY AREN'T GOLDEN…'
'OK. I'LL TRY AGAIN…'

BLUE STARS
STARS OF BETHLEHEM?
NO, NO, NO
I'LL TRY AGAIN.

RED STARS
STARS OF BETHLEHEM?
NO, NO, NO
I'LL TRY AGAIN.

HIS WHITE HORSE JUMPS AND JUMPS: "ONE, TWO, THREE…" UNTIL HE FINISHES.

HE SEES A BIG PURPLE LIGHT, A SMALL BLUE ONE, AND A SMALL RED ONE. HE IS JUMPING WITH HIS TIRELESS HORSE. THEY CAN JUMP AND JUMP ALL OF THEM. THEY ARE NOT THE STAR OF BETHLEHEM.

PURPLE, RED AND BLUE
STARS OF BETHLEHEM?
NO, NO, NO
I'LL TRY AGAIN.

HIS HORSE IS VERY TIRED AND THE SMALL BOY IS TIRED TOO. THEY ARE ON THE FRESH GRASS WHERE IT ISN'T COLD OR HOT AND THEY FALL ASLEEP. FINALLY HE CAN SEE THE BETHLEHEM STAR AND THE THREE WISE MEN. THEY HAVE GOT A BIG BAG OF PRESETS.
NEXT DAY THERE WERE PRESENTS FOR EVERYBODY.

THE THREE WISE MEN
YES, YES, YES
STAR OF BETHLEHEM
AND PRESENTS FOR YOU.
HOURRAY! HOURRAY!

LET'S COUNT THE STARS

THE THREE WISE MEN
EMOTION, EMOTION
I CAN SLEEP
LET'S COUNT THE STARS.

BLUE STARS
STARS OF BETHLEHEM?
NO, NO, NO
I'LL TRY AGAIN.
RED STARS
STARS OF BETHLEHEM?
NO, NO, NO
I'LL TRY AGAIN.

PURPLE, RED AND BLUE
STARS OF BETHLEHEM?
NO, NO, NO
I'LL TRY AGAIN.

THE THREE WISE MEN
YES, YES, YES
STAR OF BETHLEHEM
AND PRESENTS FOR YOU.
HOURRAY! HOURRAY!

TICKLING SENSATION AND ROLLING EGGS
(EASTER)

THAT EASTER HOLIDAY THE FAMILY OF RABBITS TAKES A
NAP IN THE GARDEN EVERY DAY. THEY HAVE GOT EASTER EGGS FOR CHILDREN. THE SMALLER RABBIT SLEEPS FIVE MINUTES. HE GETS BORED. HE ROLLS EGGS AND CHASES THEM.

EASTER RABBIT,
EASTER RABBIT
ROLL, ROLL, ROLL
CLAP, CLAP, CLAP.

WHEN HE IS TIRED HE TICKLES HIS DAD, HIS MUM AND
HIS BROTHERS. WITH HIS TAIL:" PUSS PUSS PUSS".
HE TICKLES THEIR NOSES. THEY SMELL:
'WHAT'S THAT? GO AWAY!'
THEY CHANGE THEIR POSITION.
THE SMALL RABBIT TICKLES THEM AGAIN.
'OH! OUT!'

EASTER RABBIT
EASTER RABBIT
TICKLE, TICKLE, TICKLE
CLAP, CLAP, CLAP.

EASTER RABBIT
EASTER RABBIT
SMELL, SMELL, SMELL
CLAP, CLAP, CLAP.

EVERY DAY THE SAME STORY, A SESSION OF TICKLING FOR HALF AN HOUR. IT'S THE BEST TIME OF THE DAY FOR THE SMALL RABBIT, BUT THE MEMBERS OF HIS FAMILY ARE TIRED AND DECIDE TO TAKE REVENGE.
EVERYONE HIDES A SPICY SPRAY.
WHEN THE SMALL RABBIT TRIES TO TICKLE WITH HIS TAIL:" PUSS, PUSS, PUSS!"
'OH! WHAT A PAIN IN MY BUM!'
ALL THE AFTERNOON THE SMALL RABBIT IS RUNNING.
THE REST OF THE FAMILY CAN TAKE A LONG NAP.

EASTER RABBIT
EASTER RABBIT
RUN, RUN, RUN
STAMP, STAMP, STAMP.
HAPPY EASTER,
HAPPY EASTER EVERYONE.

EASTER RABBIT

EASTER RABBIT
EASTER RABBIT
ROLL, ROLL, ROLL,
CLAP, CLAP, CLAP.

EASTER RABBIT
EASTER RABBIT
TICKLE, TICKLE, TICKLE
CLAP, CLAP, CLAP.

EASTER RABBIT
EASTER RABBIT
SMELL, SMELL, SMELL
CLAP, CLAP, CLAP.

EASTER RABBIT
EASTER RABBIT
RUN, RUN, RUN
STAMP, STAMP, STAMP.
HAPPY EASTER,
HAPPY EASTER EVERYONE.

THE DINOSAUR ISLAND
(ANIMALS)

A SMALL DOG WENT TO THE BEACH. HE WANTED TO PLAY. HE SWIMS AND SWIMS FOR A LONG TIME TO A NEW AND UNKNOWN ISLAND: THE DINOSAURS' ISLAND.

'THEY CAN BITE YOU,' SAYS A CORYTHOSAURUS MAKING FUN OF HIM. 'HERE YOU ARE A TYRANNOSAURUS.'

'AUGH!' ROARS THE TYRANNOSAURUS.

SMALL DOG, SMALL DOG
SWIM, SWIM, SWIM
THE DINOSAURS ISLAND
OH NO! OH NO!

THE DINOSAURS

CORYTHOSAURUS   DOG

TYRANNOSAURUS REX

THE DOG RUNS AWAY QUICKLY. HE FINDS THE VELOCIRAPTORS THAT THE TYRANNOSAURUS IS CHASING.
THE DOG RUNS AWAY. THE VELOCIRAPTORS AND THE TYRANNOSAURUS GO ON RUNNING.

DOG, DOG, DOG
RUN, RUN, RUN
TYRANNOSAURUS
CHASING, CHASING
VELOCIRAPTOR
RUN, RUN, RUN.

VELOCIRAPTORS   TYRANNOSAURUS

A BRACHIOSAURUS TALKS TO HIM:
'WHAT ARE YOU DOING HERE? CAN I HELP YOU?'
ASKS THE BRACHIOSAURUS.
'I'M LOST…'
'YOU MUST GO HOME IMMEDIATELY. YOUR PARENTS
CAN BE WORRIED.'
HIS FRIENDS, THE MARINE DINOSAURS, HELP THE
SMALL DOG TO RETURN HOME. IT IS A DIFFICULT TRIP.
THERE WAS A TERRIBLE ELASMOSAUSIUS CHASING
THEM.

BRACHIOSAURUS
HELP, HELP, HELP
MARINE DINOSAURS
SWIM, SWIM, SWIM
ELASMOSAURUS
RUN, RUN, RUN.

BRACHIOSAURUS   DOG

ELASMOSAURUS   MARINE DINOSAURS

Arqueopterix
Ornitomino
Velociraptor
Gallimino
Alosaurio
Diplodocus
Amargasaurio
Tiranosaurio
Mamenquisaurio
Tecodontosaurio
Braquiosaurio
Deimonicus
Espinosaurio

THE SMALL DOG EXPLAINS HIS HORRIBLE ADVENTURE
TO HIS PARENTS. HIS PARENTS ARE VERY ANGRY
AND VERY WORRIED.
THE SMALL DOG CHANGED HIS BEHAVIOUR AND THEY
LIVED HAPPILY EVER AFTER.

MUM AND DAD
ANGRY, ANGRY,
GOOD BEHAVIOUR
ONE, TWO, THREE.

THE LOST DOG

SMALL DOG, SMALL DOG
SWIM, SWIM, SWIM
THE DINOSAURS ISLAND
OH NO! OH NO!

DOG, DOG, DOG
RUN, RUN, RUN
TYRANNOSAURUS
CHASING, CHASING
VELOCIRAPTORS
RUN, RUN, RUN.

BRACHIOSAURUS
HELP, HEP, HELP
MARINE DINOSAURS
SWIM, SWIM, SWIM
ELASMOSAURUS
RUN, RUN, RUN.

MUM AND DAD
ANGRY, ANGRY,
GOOD BEHAVIOUR
ONE, TWO, THREE.

EAT EVERYTHING!
(FOOD)

MARIA ALWAYS ATE EVERYTHING. BUT ONCE SHE WENT TO THE BAKER'S WITH MUM. SHE SAW SOME CUPCAKES, AND SHE WANTED TO HAVE ONE…
'ONE CUPCAKE, MUM, PLEASE,'
'HERE YOU ARE,' SAID THE BAKER.
MUM BOUGHT A KILO OF CUPCAKES.
'DELICIOUS! ANOTHER ONE, MUM, PLEASE…'
MUM BOUGHT ANOTHER KILO OF CUPCAKES AND SHE GAVE HER ANOTHER ONE.

CUPCAKE, MUM, PLEASE,
YES, HERE YOU ARE!
DELICIOUS!
YAM! YAM! YAM!

BAKER

CUPCAKE

AT HOME MARIA ATE THREE MORE CUPCAKES. MUM GOT ANGRY.
'SORRY, MUM, I WAS TERRIBLY HUNGRY…'
THEN DAD ARRIVED HOME AND THEY HAD LUNCH, SPAGHETTI, MARIA'S FAVOURITE FOOD, BUT SHE COULDN'T EAT IT. HER TUMMY HURT. MUM GOT ANGRY.
'YOU MUSTN'T EAT CUPCAKES…'

MORE CUPCAKES
OH NO! OH NO!
SPAGHETTI,
NO, NO, NO,
MY TUMMY
OH NO! OH NO!

MARIA COULDN'T HAVE HER AFTERNOON SANDWICH.
SHE DIDN'T HAVE DINNER, ONLY A GLASS OF MILK.
THE NEXT DAY GRANNY CAME HOME AND SHE
LOOKED AFTER HER WHILE MUM WAS WORKING.
MARIA ATE MORE CUPCAKES.
THERE WAS RICE FOR LUNCH, BUT SHE COULDN'T
EAT IT. SHE DRANK FIZZY DRINK. HER TUMMY HURT.
SHE HAD GOT TERRIBLE DIARRHOEA AND A STOMACH
ACHE.

RICE, RICE
NO, NO, NO,
CUPCAKES AND FIZZY DRINK
OH NO! OH NO!

THEY WENT TO THE DOCTOR.
'WHAT DID YOU EAT?'
'CUPCAKES.'
'HOW MANY CUPCAKES?'
'LOTS OF CUPCAKES… AND I DRANK FIZZY DRINK.'
SHE TOOK A MEDICINE AND SHE DIDN'T EAT CUPCAKES OR DRANK FIZZY DRINK FOR A WEEK. FINALLY, SHE GOT BETTER. THEN MUM GAVE HER A CUPCAKE WITH MILK FOR BREAKFAST.
'NO, NO, NO…' SAID MARIA. 'IT'S BAD.'
'YOU CAN HAVE IT,' SAID MUM. 'YOU MUST EAT EVERYTHING BUT MODERATELY…'
AND THEY LIVED HAPPILY EVER AFTER.

EAT EVERYTHING
YES, YES, YES
YOU ARE HAPPY
ONE, TWO, THREE.

EAT EVERYTHING!

CUPCAKE, MUM, PLEASE,
YES, HERE YOU ARE!
DELICIOUS!
YAM! YAM! YAM!

MORE CUPCAKES
OH NO! OH NO!
SPAGHETTI,
NO, NO, NO,
MY TUMMY
OH NO! OH NO

RICE, RICE
NO, NO, NO,
CUPCAKES AND FIZZY DRINK
OH NO! OH NO!

EAT EVERYTHING
YES, YES, YES
YOU ARE HAPPY
ONE, TWO, THREE.

CAN I HELP YOU?
(ATTITUDE)

ONCE UPON A TIME THERE WAS A DOG WALKING ON
THE BEACH. HE FISHED UNDER ROCKS.
THERE WAS SOMETHING BLACK IN THE WATER.
'HELLO,' SAID THE WHALE.
'HELLO,' SAID THE DOG.
'I'M A LITTLE WHALE. I'M LOST…'
'WHERE IS YOUR MOTHER?'
'I DON'T KNOW'
'CAN I HELP YOU? ' ASKED THE DOG.
'YES, I MUST FIND MY MOTHER.
'LET'S SWIM TO YOUR MOTHER,' SAID THE DOG.

DOG, DOG, DOG
HELP, HELP, HELP
WHALE, WHALE
LOST, LOST, LOST.

THE DOG HELPED HER. THEY SWAM AND SWAM TOGETHER UNTIL THEY FOUND HER MOTHER AND SISTERS.
'MUM!'
'SWEET!' ARE YOU OK?'
'YES, I AM,' SAID THE LITTLE WHALE. 'THIS FRIEND HELPED ME…'

HELP, HELP, HELP
YES, YES, YES
MOTHER AND SISTERS
HAPPY, HAPPY, HAPPY.

'THANK YOU,' SAID MUM. 'CAN I HELP YOU?'
'YES,' SAID THE DOG. 'I'M VERY TIRED. I CAN'T GET BACK HOME…'
MUM WHALE CARRIED THE DOG ON HER BACK AND SHE SWAM AS FAR AS THE COASTLINE. HER DAUGHTERS FOLLOWED THEM.

GET BACK HOME
YES, YES, YES
THE DOG ON THE WHALE
ONE, TWO, THREE.

'BYE-BYE AND THANKS,' SAID THE WHALES.
'BYE-BYE. SEE YOU,' SAID THE DOG. 'NICE TO MEET YOU.'   'SEE YOU TOMORROW?' SAID THE SMALL WHALE.
'OK,' SAID THE DOG.
THE WHALE AND THE DOG PLAYED TOGETHER FOR YEARS. AND THEY LIVED HAPPILY EVER AFTER.

BYE- BYE, BYE- BYE
SEE YOU TOMORROW
YOU ARE MY FRIEND
ONE, TWO, THREE.

CAN I HELP YOU?

DOG, DOG, DOG
HELP, HELP, HELP
WHALE, WHALE
LOST, LOST, LOST

HELP, HELP, HELP
YES, YES, YES
MOTHER AND SISTERS
HAPPY, HAPPY, HAPPY.

GET BACK HOME
YES, YES, YES
THE DOG ON THE WHALE
ONE, TWO, THREE.

BYE-BYE, BYE-BYE
SEE YOU TOMORROW
YOU ARE MY FRIEND
ONE, TWO, THREE.